Leading Like a Lady: How ...

PUBLISHED BY DOYENNE LEADERSHIP INSTITUTE, LLC
4920 West Baseline Road, Suite 105-211
Laveen, Arizona 85339
www.DoyenneLeadership.com

ISBN 978-0-9895295-0-1
ISBN 978-0-9895295-1-8 (electronic)

Copyright © 2013 by Nadia Brown
Cover design by Lawrence Riddick

Printed in the United States of America

Dedication

This book is dedicated to three future leading ladies: DeShanae Bell, Dai'jah Hunter, and Aryahn Brown.

Acknowledgements

Special thanks to all of the women who participated in this book project by sharing their stories.

I would also like to thank my amazing support team, Adrienne Montgomery, LaToya Rosario, Lawrence Riddick. This project was possible because of your support and dedication. Thanks to the ladies of Positioned for Promises (P4P) Stellina Yarbrough, Joy McClain, Noel McClain and Kendra Johnson. My sister friend Shakena Ravnell and last but not least my wonderful husband, Toby Brown.

Table of Contents

Introduction

All too often in my work, I watch women take themselves out of the leadership equation. Sadly, women do not perceive themselves as leaders, because they make it appear more difficult than it is or they believe in a mystical concept that they must first achieve a certain title to be a leader. This perception is so far from the truth.

One of my favorite definitions of leadership comes from Ken Blanchard and Phil Hodges who defined leadership as "anytime you seek to influence the thinking, behavior, or development of people toward accomplishing a goal in their personal or professional lives you are taking on the role of a leader." [1]

The fact is leadership begins before you get the title. There are key steps that you can take no matter where you are in your career to position yourself for the role that you want.

Additional challenges that halt or stall women from entering their roles as leaders is viewing leadership through an outdated paradigm and not being able to develop their own unique leadership style and approach. The former leadership paradigm consisted mostly of a "command-and-control approach" where orders were passed down from the top. [2]

However, what once worked so well in more production or manufacturing-based environments is ill-suited for today's innovative organizations where change is the only thing that is truly consistent. Now, collaboration and teamwork are highly valued assets toward increasing the bottom line. In this new leadership paradigm, women can lead like a lady without taking on the personalities of men or being bossy. When you are leading like a lady, you can be yourself and still handle business effectively.

All employees at all levels of the organization are expected to demonstrate leadership qualities, such as having integrity, being decisive, exercising discipline, showing drive, and demonstrating influence. These attributes also are connected to being a woman leader. Therefore, no matter what your current title may be, you are a leader.

"You are a leader, long before you get the title."

So, you might be seeing the word "title" and think that this book is about climbing the corporate ladder. Actually, I am not trying to convince you to climb the corporate ladder if it is not your dream. The purpose of *Leading Like a Lady* is to awaken and empower the woman leader within you to accomplish your career desires whatever they may be.

What is the dream that you have? I understand that every woman does not want to be the CEO of a Fortune 500 company. Perhaps you want to start your own business, become a housewife, or go build schools in Africa. Also, it is possible that you enjoy your current job role and want to expand your sphere of influence or become more effective in your position. No matter what your current title is you are a leader, and you own the power to make your dream a reality.

What's In a Name?

My company name is Doyenne Leadership Institute. I often am asked, what does Doyenne (pronounced doi-en) mean? When thinking about my company name, I wanted a word that captured the essence of what women leaders should feel in their roles.

Doyenne means "a prominent woman in a particular field; a woman considered to be knowledgeable or uniquely skilled as a result of long experience in some field or endeavor."[3]

I know that is a huge mouth full and plenty to chew on! But it all boils down to one word that really stood out the most for me: prominent. According to Merriam-Webster's dictionary, prominent means "standing out." And that is what you are meant to be—a "stand out" woman leader.

In my favorite quote by Marianne Williamson, she said, "Your playing small does not serve the world. There is nothing enlightening about shrinking so that other people won't feel insecure around you … as we let our light shine we unconsciously give other people permission to do the same." A standout woman leader or Doyenne, does not play small. She comes out of the shadows and owns the essence of her gifts and talents and her role as a leader. She possesses three key characteristics. She is authentic. She is confident. She is strong.

You Can't Afford to Blend

As a Doyenne, blending in or hiding is not an option. No matter how tempting it may be to blend in within your organization, it could be detrimental to your career ascension and achieving your dreams. You must resist the temptation and seek opportunities to stand out and have your voice and ideas heard.

As women, we were taught it is not ladylike to toot our own horns. In fact, if someone did toot our horn for us, we refuse, deflect, or down play the accolade. "Oh, that was nothing." Consequently, we remain silent. Our silence can cause us to get stuck in a position or organization. Down playing your gifts and successes will not help you advance your career. Remember: You are a Doyenne now. You are prominent, knowledgeable, and uniquely skilled. It is time you acknowledged your worth and shared it with others.

Executives and managers in today's organizations are very busy, and it is your responsibility to ensure that not only is your leadership aware of your accomplishments, but they are also aware of your career goals and aspirations. Beware of falling into the trap of thinking that your accomplishments will speak for themselves. While hard work is a given, you must make sure that your accomplishments are known. Please understand I am not instructing you to be a prideful big shot. There is a difference between pride and confidence. I am encouraging a purposeful confidence that is characteristic of a leader.

A practical method for tracking your successes is keeping what I call a kudos folder. Whether through an electronic or paper file, this folder keeps an ongoing tab of what you have achieved and positive customer feedback you have received throughout the year. Use this folder as a reminder to share with your managers why you are a great leader in your department and organization. Barbara, a director with a major financial institution, shared that a key to shattering her inner glass ceiling was ensuring her voice was heard. She had to believe that what she had to offer was "valuable, needed, and worth hearing." One way to do this is to prepare a weekly status sheet that you share with your leader during your regular one-on-one meetings.

Why Leading Like a Lady?

It is tempting to hear the title Leading Like a Lady and

immediately think weaker or lesser. After all, we are often told that women are the "weaker" sex, and I believe that this notion has been taken to the extreme. When I use to hear the word "lady," I would picture a dainty, refined woman who would never consider herself to be a leader and might be called a doormat. However, after conducting my graduate research and working among amazing woman leaders, my perspective shifted.

A few of the definitions for the word lady from Merriam-Webster Collegiate Dictionary are "a woman who is refined, polite, and well-spoken; a woman having proprietary rights or authority especially as a feudal superior; and a woman of superior social position."[4] Rights. Superior. Authority. Those words do not sound weak to me. It actually puts me in mind of a Doyenne.

Leading like a lady is a call to action for women leaders to be:

- **authentic**, because they have developed their own unique leadership style. They are not trying to lead like anyone else, especially men by taking on more male characteristics, which tends to back fire and alienate others.

- **confident** in their unique gifts, talents, skills, and abilities. They are not arrogant, but have an unshakeable assuredness in their ability to perform and lead well. They are confident enough to take calculated risks and will take action even when afraid.

- **strong**, because they have developed strong leadership skills and attributes. These leaders know where to go to ask for help and are comfortable asking for help when needed. They realize that they cannot do it all and understand the power of delegation and asking relevant questions. They are committed to building up their team members and themselves. A part of being strong includes paying attention to their physical health, making sure to get proper rest, and taking a vacation as needed.

The journey to leading like a lady is worth it. It is a journey of struggle and triumph to break old habits, to believe new truths, to trust in the unknown, and to follow your own divine course. Von, a senior vice president with a major bank, shared that she had to remind herself that the journey will not be easy. When she started out and looked at other successful people, they all made it look easy. It appeared as if they knew everything, but "the reality is nobody knows everything and nothing worth having really comes out easily." I agree that we all have to remind ourselves of that sometimes.

In the proceeding chapters, I will empower you to acknowledge and break through the internal glass barriers that are standing in the way of your career success and advancement. Are you ready? For the next step you might want a sledgehammer.

The Glass Ceiling: Is it a Myth?

The glass ceiling as defined by Hesse-Biber and Carter (2005) is an invisible barrier that prevents women and minorities from ascending into more powerful or prestigious roles within organizations, which in turn often causes qualified candidates to feel unworthy of occupying such positions.[5] There is some debate around when the term was first used.

However, the term became popular in 1986 after a Wall Street Journal article by Carol Hymowitz and Timothy Schellhardt.[6] After that the glass ceiling began to become prominent getting presidential attention. The Department of Labor issued a report on the Glass Ceiling Initiative in 1991 prompting then-President George H.W. Bush to appoint a bipartisan committee to identify the barriers of the glass ceiling.[7]

When I was first asked if I thought the glass ceiling was merely a myth, my first response was adamantly, "No!" How could the barrier that has held so many women back from reaching the top only be a myth? Surely, it was true. After all, I had conducted my doctoral research on the topic and all of the women interviewed resoundingly said, "Yes!" For those women it was the glass ceiling that had impacted their careers in some way, usually negative. Whether it was in terms of advancement, pay or both, the glass ceiling was firmly intact and getting plenty of attention. But what if we have been putting the blame on a myth?

What Is a Myth?

The dictionary defines myth as "a false collective belief that is used to justify a social institution." Notice it is a false belief. The glass ceiling simply does not exist. It only exists in our minds, because we have been told for so long that it is there.

If we look at the numbers, it seems that nationally women leaders are breaking through the glass ceiling and going higher than ever in history. Research shows that women now hold nearly half of America's jobs, earn nearly 60 percent of all bachelor's and master's degrees, and hold nearly 51 percent of managerial and professional positions.[8] In 2009, women earned more doctoral credentials than men for the first time in history. The numbers are similar in the United Kingdom as well.[9]

Additionally, the numbers are steadily rising in the ranks right below the CEO level. More women are now earning $100,000 or more annually than ever before. In 2009, approximately one in 18 women earned $100,000 or more, which signified a 14 percent increase in over two years. Over the past 20 years the number of women occupying positions that were previously only held by men has steadily increased. However, when it comes to the most senior-level executive positions, the number of women is dismal with only

4 percent of Fortune 500 companies being led by female CEOs in 2012.[10]

What is really going on? The statistics show that the corporate climate is changing. Not only is the number of women rising in the ranks, but the understanding of their value and impact to the bottom line has increased among their colleagues and leaders. Yet still many women feel their career dreams and aspirations are doomed to collide with the glass ceiling. What is the truth behind why women still feel that their careers are being hindered?

The Real Glass Ceiling

For years, we, as women have been told of this invisible glass ceiling that has been limiting our ability to advance and achieve our dreams.

Carter G. Woodson wrote:

> **If you can control a man's thinking you do not have to worry about his action. When you determine what a man shall think you do not have to concern yourself about what he will do. If you make a man feel that he is inferior, you do not have to compel him to accept an inferior status, for he will seek it himself. If you make a man think that he is justly an outcast, you do not have to order him to the back door. He will go without being told; and if there is no back door, his very nature will demand one.[11]**

For years, we have been told about this glass ceiling that is standing in the way of our career progress. Since 1991, the glass ceiling started to take the shape of a house. There is now more mythical glass than ever. Glass walls have shown up that prevent women from making various lateral moves within organizations.[12] Finally, there is the glass cliff which Ryan and Haslam define as the "phenomenon where women [or members of other minority groups] are more likely to be found in leadership positions that are associated with a greater risk of failure and criticism."[13]

Woodson is right. We bought into the lies that there was this ceiling holding us back. We accepted the myth that there were these forces external to us preventing us from achieving our goals. The glass ceiling began to control our thinking and then, our actions. Ultimately, we have trapped ourselves in a designer glass cage blaming everyone and everything for our lack of career progress, because we have bought into the lies. We allowed the experts and others to make us to feel inferior as if somehow we did not have the goods. And in doing so, there is no need for anyone to erect a glass ceiling, glass walls, or a glass cliff, because we have willingly settled into the glass cages on our own.

The truth is the true glass ceiling is the one within us. It is a lack of confidence, which prevents you from going after your dreams. It is that voice that constantly tells you that you are not good enough, pretty enough, smart enough, or ambitious enough to make it to the top.

Rosin reported that the women of Silicon Valley see sexism as "an omnipresent and unpleasant fact of life, but it shouldn't keep you from going about your business" or pursuing your goals.[14] Continuing to focus on the external distracts you from not only your goal, but the internal barriers that you must overcome. While there are plenty of external barriers about which to be concerned, there are many more internal barriers we, as women leaders, have the power to overcome.

Ginni Rometty, CEO of IBM, shared a story of an experience that she had early in her career. She was offered a significant opportunity.[15] You know, one of those mega opportunities that do not come around every day. She shared that she immediately said that she was not ready and that she needed more time. Ginni told the hiring manager that she needed to think about it and respond back tomorrow.

Later that evening she relayed the story to her husband. When she was done, Ginni's husband looked at her and said, "Do you think a man would have responded to that question that way?" He then continued to encourage her to take the position, because he knew that she could do the position. The challenge would be great, and she would not get bored.

Think about Ginni's story. She was being offered an incredible chance to move up toward her dream. There was no external glass ceiling waiting to drop down on her head. No. It was Ginni's inner glass ceiling that was putting limits on her. What about your life? What opportunities have you been offered that you hesitated and pondered instead of taking the confident step toward your dream?

A 2011 study by Europe's Institute of Leadership and Management (ILM) revealed that women's careers were "hindered by lower expectations and ambitions" due to a lack of self-belief and confidence.[16] This lack of confidence led to having lower ambitions and expectations than their male colleagues. As a result, women obtain managerial or leadership roles an average of three years later than their male counterparts. Wow! Are you willing to settle for a three-year delay on achieving your goals? I know I am not. Pick up that sledgehammer and start shattering your own inner glass ceiling. It has been causing you to lose out on time, happiness, health, and wealth. You should not pay that cost.

What is it Costing You?

Women also are less likely to negotiate their salaries. A 2003 study published in the Harvard Business Review showed that only 7 percent of female graduates attempted to negotiate their salaries in comparison to 57 percent of their male counterparts.[17] That means a whopping 93 percent of women did not even try! The fact that men negotiated their salaries resulted in men having a starting salary that was 7.6 percent higher than women.[18]

I was one of those female graduates. When I received my first offer as a new college graduate, my hiring manager made an offer (a fair one I might add) and I gleefully accepted. I was so excited. With six months till graduation, I had already received a job offer. That meant I could finish the last two semesters of school without that hanging over my head.

However, I did not consider what would happen when I decided to leave that position. How would I negotiate my next salary? I did not think about the fact that the salary negotiations at the next position would sometimes begin with maneuvering the question about my current salary. If my current salary was not up to par, it did not make it easier to handle future salary negotiations. According to Babcock, because of this increased start, all things being considered equal and the man and woman both received the same increases over the years, the man's 7.6 percent difference in salary increase would result in him making more than $360,000 more over 38 years than his female counterpart.[19]

As a female leader, Peatric cringes at the notion of women who do not recognize their worth as leaders. She said that women often short change themselves, particularly when it comes to negotiating their salaries. "I've seen men negotiating their salary and they didn't even have a degree." Part of this is because a number of women are uncomfortable recognizing and identifying their worth during salary negotiations. However, men do not seem to have that issue. Because Peatric has held managerial positions, she has taken the initiative to help level the playing field. "I've taken roles and was appalled at how little some of my female team members were being paid. I've gone in and made adjustments to their salaries, because they simply were underpaid," she said. As a woman, Peatric knew that their pay was not equitable and since she was in the position to make a difference, she did something about it.

Peatric gave reassuring advice: Women need to realize that when an organization really wants you, they will make it work. In negotiating her own pay, Peatric has told organizational leaders, "Financially I need to be [at this salary], and I cannot go below this." In each case, the company met her asking salary with no problem.

You must be prepared when entering salary negotiations. Do your homework by researching the company, the area, and the comparable salaries. Take into consideration your work experience, length of experience, degrees, and certifications. Practice asking for the amount you want ahead of time and be prepared to clearly justify it if necessary. Also, remember that salary is only a piece of the pie. Consider negotiating other benefits such as flex-time, paid-time off, signing bonuses, and stock options.

Not only is there an actual financial cost to believing in the glass-ceiling myth, there is also the physical cost. I have spoken with some women who say it is not all about the money. For many women that is true. There are studies that support this by revealing that women often have different motivators. However, the lack of confidence leads to increased stress. According to Collette Dowling, MSW a lack of confidence is the number one reason why women seek help from psychotherapists.[20]

The Glass Wall of FEAR

What if the glass ceiling, glass wall, and glass cliff are true? Many times what is holding us back is the influx of what-if questions flooding our mind. What if I say this, and people get angry? What if I pursue this position, and I lose my friends, spouse, or children? What if I confront that mean girl, and she retaliates? What if? What if? What if?

Oftentimes, we do not want to admit that fear is really what is holding us back. In some cases, we do not even realize that it is fear. When working with my clients, fear often shows up as procrastination, inability to make decisions, or unproductive busyness. They often busy themselves doing things that are non-threatening or sometimes unimportant to distract them from addressing the issues or tasks that truly need to be handled.

Fear is defined as "a distressing emotion aroused by impending danger, evil, or pain whether the threat is real or imagined." Other terms for fear are apprehension, dismay, dread, or terror. Can you relate? Is a person or task keeping you awake at night and dreading the arrival of the next day? I want to point out that that fear can occur in the same manner whether the threat is real or imagined.

As a leader, you will have to do things that take you out of your comfort zone. For some of us, the thought of handling certain situations causes us to freeze or become paralyzed. Maybe it is speaking in front of a crowd or taking a firm stance against a new company policy. However, when it comes to fear, your body will respond the same when it is merely a thought or idea holding you back versus an actual, tangible threat.

I live in the beautiful city of Phoenix, Arizona, and while I absolutely love living here, I think we have some of the worst drivers on the planet! Although that may be a slight exaggeration, I have had the opportunity to experience a real threat—evoked threat that evoked fear. Recently, while riding in the car with my husband driving, one fellow Phoenician driver decided that it was OK to run a red light right in front of our car. In rapid response, my husband had to slam on the brakes to avoid a collision. You can imagine my heart was racing as I realized how close we had come to being hurt.

Pause for a moment and think about a recent incident that produced fear in your mind and body. It may have been today or yesterday or sometime in the past. Think about how your body reacted: heart racing, shortness of breath, sweaty palms, or shaking limbs. You were scared and rightfully so!

Similar things happen even when the threat is not real. Many years ago, I heard this acronym to describe fear: False Evidence Appearing Real. How many times have we been so upset or worried about the mere possibility of something happening only to have it not happen at all?

Fear makes the wolf bigger than it is!
German Proverb

When coaching women leaders, my follow-up question to their what-if questions is, "What's the worst thing that can happen? What if you apply for that senior-level position and get rejected? What if you have that difficult conversation and the person gets upset? What is the worst thing that can happen? For me, my gauge is that the worst thing that can happen is that I die. Therefore, I alter that what-if question and ask, "If I apply for this position and I am not selected, will I die?" Of course, they answer is no. "If I have this difficult conversation and the other person gets upset, will I die?" Again, the answer is no. Therefore, when I reframe the question and the answer is no, then despite how I may feel, I do the task anyway. I send the email; I make the sales or follow-up call; and I host the training webinar. I do whatever it is that I was "what-iffing" about, and in doing so I get the courage and confidence to do it again.

The Impostor Syndrome

Dr. Valerie Young, author of *The Secret Thoughts of Successful Women,* addresses the impostor syndrome, which "refers to people who have a persistent belief in their lack of intelligence, skills, or competence." These impostors are "convinced that other people's praise and recognition of their accomplishments is undeserved, chalking up their achievements to chance, charm, connections, and other external factors." Although many men suffer from the impostor syndrome, it is believed that women are impacted by it more.[21]

Dr. Young explains that the impostor syndrome is not simply another word for low self-esteem or a lack of confidence, but it references the fear and anxiety caused by a nagging self-doubt. "I am not as good as I should be." You often find ways to explain or minimize your success and accomplishments. In the case of the impostor syndrome, more success actually breeds more self-doubt. Instead of success validating your skills and abilities, it increases the pressure and anxiety because you now feel that you somehow fooled people to achieve this. You may ask yourself questions, such as, "How did this happen? Did I pay enough dues? Do I deserve to be here?"

I can completely relate to this. After years of school and increasing advancement, I often struggled with my success often to the point of not even wanting to talk about it. I recall when I completed my doctoral degree, my husband was the one who shared the news the most. While I was relieved that it was over and proud that I had stuck it out, part of me wondered if that was enough. Maybe I should go back and get another degree to prove that the first three were not some sort of fluke. Really?

It did not stop there. I was most affected by the impostor syndrome when I decided to branch out and start my own business, which involves speaking, training, and coaching. Suddenly, not only am I now striving to be a successful business woman, but I am doing so in a very visible way. I remember the anxiety and worry before every workshop presentation and webinar when no one could see me. Afterward when people would give me accolades, I would secretly wonder if I could continue to live up to those expectations. What if my success was only a fluke and I really was not as good as I thought?

Dealing with Insecurity

Feelings of fear and insecurity are almost a given when moving up in your career. However, they do not have to reign supreme, and you can excel past them. It helps to be prepared to experience feelings of insecurity, uncertainty, doubt, and fear so that you do not allow them to prevent you from moving forward.

Von, a senior vice president at a large financial institution, shared a story from earlier in her career. She shared that she was approached by a senior level manager to take on a role as his market administrator. In speaking with him it sounded like an exciting assignment; however, it was a lower pay grade. Von was unsure about taking it, because it appeared as if she would be taking a step backward instead of taking a step forward. At this time in her career, she was actually managing a team of about 10 people, but in the proposed position, she would have no direct reports. So, she turned it down.

Months later, the same senior-level manager approached Von a second time regarding the same position. However, this time he had been promoted and had more market share than before. Because of this, Von accepted the job, but felt insecure in the role for a number of reasons. One of her initial insecurities was around expectations. Von was not clear on what was expected of her in the new role, and she was struggling with the shift from having 10 direct reports to none. She shared that felt she was moving out of management and was not sure how that would impact her career. Although she was not an assistant in the market administrator role, Von thought the outward perception was that she was a woman reporting to a male manager. Overcoming those feelings was no easy task.

Next, Von felt insecure about what she was doing and learning in her new job. Every new job requires one to learn new things. Von asserts that as long as you are growing and changing, it can be good for your career. When you take on new roles, there is no expectation that you will have to know it all in a day. However it is good to communicate with your leadership about their expectations so that you are both on the same page.

Lastly, Von dealt with feelings of insecurity around what came next in her career. There was no clear career path for her current division and her role as market administrator. What would come next for her once her time in this position was done? Von stayed in the position for four years and eventually managed a small team of people. She shared, "I loved that role and learned a ton." Ultimately, she left the role and the bank because it did not provide the level of job security that she once felt. One of the things that she has learned to deal with in her career was the many ebbs and flows in the financial industry that can lead to layoffs.

From Von's story, it is clear that insecurity, doubt, and fear are not to be taken as stop signs in your career. It is actually a normal part of the journey similar to encountering detours or construction on a road trip. Instead of canceling the road trip, you navigate around or through the issues. Von shared, "You can have these feelings of insecurity at any point [in your career] even when you are moving up, because all of a sudden you are a smaller fish in a bigger pond where you once were a bigger fish in a smaller pond. Now, people are expecting things of you and you don't know what that means, and you have to play differently."

When asked to share how she overcame those feelings of insecurity, particularly when moving up in her career, Von shared that it helped for her to build relationships and have strong mentors. "I've had many really, strong leaders and mentors, but there was this one female mentor that I hugely respected. She had a good way of telling me what I did well, how I did it, how it differentiated me, and why it was unique." Von continued, "The powerful thing about that for me was it enabled me to harness that in the future."

Thanks to the input of her mentor, Von now had a weapon to dull the insecurity she felt in her new role. She could remember the positive feedback she heard in the past and used it to regain security in her strengths and abilities as a leader. Von also shared that it is important to build strong relationships when moving into a new role and it can take time to develop those relationships. Since Von thrives on building relationships, creating partnerships, and working collaboratively, it really helped her through all of her career transitions. She shared that because it takes a little while to build new relationships in your new role sometimes you need to draw upon your old relationships for a while. She added, "but you need to pretty quickly [start] building those new ones, and it can be as simple as an assistant. It doesn't always have to be a senior person. It can be anybody who can provide help and support and is willing to share their knowledge with you because when you're in a new department, anybody in that department knows more than you do."

Another key piece in overcoming insecurity is to be bold and ask questions. Building relationships and collaboration are crucial to being a leader, but you also cannot be afraid to ask questions. Many times you may be tempted to keep quiet out of fear of looking incompetent, but the effect of not asking questions could prove to be more detrimental. Von shared, "For me I just feel that asking questions is so key, and I think the most unhealthy work environment is the work environment where questions are not encouraged and valued. Because chances are if you have that question, a ton of other people do, too. So people are usually really glad that you asked the question."

When learning a new role, there is so much new information to absorb as you adjust to all of your new responsibilities. Von made a key point when she shared that sometimes in her career she has asked five different people the same question and received five different answers. It would seem this would be confusing and frustrating, but Von said that she walked away and gained a whole new perspective and understanding from the various responses.

You Own the Power

As a woman leader, you must become comfortable with owning your power and authority. Power is not only about ability, but also authority. In being an excellent leader, you must understand that your knowledge is what gives you your authority. You have worked tirelessly to not only obtain a degree (or two), but to go the extra mile (or two) to gain skills beyond your degree. That effort and knowledge makes you the expert. You are the authority and the leader. Own it.

When it comes to power, many women still struggle with the concept of using power in their leadership. It may evoke negative associations based on previous experiences with the abuse of power. However, exercising power is an essential part of leadership. Women need to become more comfortable with having and exercising their power. As a leader, power is a vital resource that unlocks success.

Casey Mulligan cites a 2009 study by the U.S. Department of Labor, which states the number of women in the workforce was greater than the number of men for the first time in history.[22] As a result of this shift in the makeup of the workforce and the shift in the nature of jobs, feminine attributes that were once seen as being more negative actually have become more valuable in the workplace. Rosin states "feminine attributes, like empathy, patience, and communal problem-solving" are beginning to replace the more top-down model of success.[23]

Additionally, in a study conducted by the Boston Consulting

Group, "globally women control nearly $12 trillion of the overall $18.4 trillion in consumer spending."[24] Not only have women made progress in organizations and academia, but they are generally the decision makers when it comes to spending in households. Who knows what women want as consumers better than women?

In a 2004 Catalyst report it was found that "companies with the highest representation of women on their top management teams experienced better financial performance than companies with the lowest women's representation."[25] Now more than ever before are women poised to breakthrough all of the external barriers that once prevented them from possessing more positions at the top.

You are not a Victim

Although, it may be tempting to play the "woe is me" song over and over while feeling sorry for yourself for the lack of movement and advancement in your career, stop it. Do not press play on that track anymore. Repeat after me: "I am not a victim." By continuing to blame others, the stock market, the economy, or your boss for your current situation, you are building that invisible glass cage and relegating your power into the hands of others. The only way to move past the disappointment of your current career stance is to take responsibility for where you are. What you see right now in your life and career is a result of your decisions. Millions of people deal with similar challenges as you every day. What can you do to directly address the issues you face? Do you need to seek a position in a new industry or maybe have a candid conversation with your manager? Whatever your circumstances are remember that you are not a victim.

By taking the position as the victim, you give up your power and your ability to address the issue. You own the power to make decisions that can change your current situation. Barbara shared that one of the keys to her success was passing the victim test. She stated, "There will be many tests, but being able to pass the victim test is key. Deal with issues at the root. Be open, honest, and direct with male and female colleagues [alike]."

The victim test is better known as "the blame game"— blaming yourself or others for the present circumstances in your life. When choosing to play the victim, you actually give away all of your power. Dr. Susan Jeffers, author of *Feel the Fear and Do It Anyway* stated, "When you blame any outside force for any of your experiences of life, you are literally giving away all your power and thus creating pain, paralysis, and depression."[26] If you are in pain, paralyzed and depressed, you are clearly not moving in the direction that you want to go in your career.

One thing to note is that taking responsibility for your life, career, actions, and decisions means not playing the blame game. This includes not blaming yourself. Acknowledge where you are and take responsibility for it. Then, devise a plan to move on and move up. Getting stuck in a cycle of blame, whether it is yourself or someone else, is counterproductive and will not empower you to move forward. Trust me, I know from personal experience.

My manager and I were at odds, again. I was so tired. I just wanted her to go away and let me do my job in peace, but that did not seem as if it was ever going to happen. Every time I turned around, or so it seemed, there was some new complaint or accusation being hurled my way, which disturbed my peace.

At first, I blamed her. I would say things like, "If she would just leave me alone, get a clue, find a new job, then I would be fine." By the time, it was all said and done, I had thought of everything short

31

of terminal illness or death to get her out of my life.

The truth is that I did not want to take responsibility for the tension in our relationship. I did not want to ask myself the tough questions like, why are you not taking the high road and addressing the elephant in the room. Why do you continue to act as if pretending there is no problem will resolve it?

There were other hard truths I needed to face, such as the fact that I was in a job that I did not like. I knew there were other things that I now wanted to do, but I had allowed fear and the blame game to keep me stuck. Just like I had the choice of whether I had a frank conversation with my boss or not, I also had a choice over whether or not I remained in this position.

But as long as it was her fault, then it was OK, because I did not have to take responsibility for my role in the matter. Once I took responsibility, acknowledged my role in the situation, devised my plan, repaired that relationship and moved forward in my career, I overcame my fear and passed the victim test.

In getting to the root of the issue, you must be willing to have open and honest communication with yourself by being direct and admitting how you feel. First, address any of the stories that you might be telling yourself. Are you saying things to yourself, such as he/she just doesn't like me or my boss is such a jerk? Is that true? How have your thoughts and feelings colored your view of your relationship and influenced your interactions with this person? Use the following steps to pass the victim test.

Take time to put yourself in the other person's shoes to see how they might see the situation. What are some of the challenges that they are facing? Are they receiving pressure from another source?

Then, have the courage to pull them aside and speak with them.

It often helps to start by asking sincere questions. If asked why you want to know, genuinely explain your reasoning and openly seek to get to the heart of the matter. Stephen Covey said, "Seek first to understand, then to be understood." The other person may or may not be ready to engage, but at least try. I know that the sooner you do this after a situation arises, the easier it is to address.

Many of the conflicts in our work and personal relationships are simple misunderstandings. When I made up my mind to do this with my manager, it worked miracles. Although I knew I was leaving, I did not want my final days to feel like I was in the midst of World War III. Amazingly, she must have made the same decision since our conversation started off with her seeking to understand and opened the door to having a genuine dialogue and discussing areas that had plagued our relationship for almost a year. Imagine how much peace I would have had if I had done that sooner.

How do I Play the Game if I Don't Know the Rules?

I remember the day I asked my now husband this very question. I was moving along in my career and was fairly ignorant of the fact that I was suffering from the "tiara syndrome" and had not paid attention to the rules of advancement. The tiara syndrome is a term coined by Debra Kolb, Ph.D. and Carol Frohlinger, J.D., the founders of Negotiating Women, Inc. The phrase refers to the phenomenon where women tend to wait for their work achievements and accomplishments to be noticed versus taking the initiative and tooting their own horn. Conversely, their male counterparts are more likely to discuss their accomplishments and negotiate for advanced positions and increased salaries.[27]

While on some level, I was aware that there were differences in the way people were treated based on gender, race, and age at some companies, I would never let that impact or sway me. However, one day it hit me in the face like a ton of bricks. Piling on top of me were these unwritten rules toward advancing in the organization, and I had no clue as to what they were! Here I was an ambitious, determined, hard-working woman with a BS and an MBA, yet my career was not moving at the pace that I thought it should.

I thought that if I continued to work hard that someone would notice my accomplishments and reward me accordingly. Boy was I wrong! Hard work and having skills are only a piece of the puzzle. As a leader, you must take charge of your career. You cannot expect anyone else to do it for you. I am reminded of a line from the movie The Pursuit of Happyness (2006) where the main character, Chris Gardner looks at his son and says, "Don't ever let somebody tell you, you can't do something. Not even me. [If] you got a dream, you gotta protect it. People can't do something they wanna tell you, you can't do it. If you want something, go get it. Period."[28]

Take off the tiara. The truth is that you must stop waiting for others to recognize your worthiness and start making it known to them. Take the initiative to advance your career. If you want that leadership position, go for it now. When my eyes were opened to this, it was so empowering. Notice I said empowering and not comfortable. Even today it is sometimes challenging to toot my own horn or speak of my accomplishments. However, if I was ever going to attain the level of success I desired, I had to step up and start playing the game.

One of the first keys to playing the game is to acknowledge that it is a game. I know when I first heard this I was justifiably upset because I did not think it was a game at all. This was my life—my livelihood. How could it possibly be a game? However, pretending it is not a game will not help you advance your career and in some cases may hinder you from being successful in your role.

Next, learn the rules to the game and understand that the rules of the game may change from organization to organization or even from department to department. Every organization has formal written rules and policies. But as leaders we have to also know about the informal and unwritten rules in workplaces. You must learn both if you desire to be successful and advance your career. Pay attention to what is taking place around you. What are others doing to be promoted? Who do you need to get to know in order to increase your executive presence? Take the time away from your desk to have lunch or a cup of coffee with colleagues and build relationships. This is a key piece to not only learning the rules, but it also helps you to build strong relationships and a strong network.

Finally, to play the game to win, you must take ownership. One of the issues Peatric has noticed with women leaders throughout her career has been how women respond to the men in the organization, including their peers. "I have a problem with women complaining and not taking ownership of [their] role," Peatric said. Also, she advises that women leaders not be moved by team members' emotions and that they focus on being really strong in the areas where they need to be. If you are going to play, then you should play to win. Remember taking initiative and being proactive are key. Sometimes it is better to ask for forgiveness than for permission. Observe Barbara's example.

Barbara recalled a time when her company was in trouble with another financial institution. To prepare for the fallout, Barbara took the initiative to prepare a response by pulling together the necessary team and data. Initially, her boss blew her off when she shared what she was doing, but she did not allow that to deter her efforts. After attending a meeting with his higher ups, he came to Barbara to get access to the information that she had pulled together. That information ultimately saved his job, and he never forgot that she did that. Later, he moved into another position, and Barbara took over his role.

Being an active player in the game will shatter your inner glass ceiling. Barbara shared that it pays to be first. "If everyone is fighting for the same position [I think to myself], how I can create my own opportunity?" She advised, "Take the risks, be first, get it done, and let the results speak for [themselves]."

Remember, if you do not play the game, then you will get played.

Crush the Lies & Know the True You

Who are you? I am not talking about who your mama said you are. Not who your daddy said you are. Not your best friend from second grade. Not your ex-boyfriend. Your husband or even who society says you are. But, who do you say you are?

Who are you behind the mask? Behind the perfect hair, the corporate suite, the Jimmy Choo shoes, the pasted on smile, or the icy chill? Who are you?

Face it: Being a woman in leadership comes with its own unique challenges. Depending on the organization it may be challenging to be yourself or fully embrace your femininity and your special gifts.

Who are you really? Do you even know how to answer that question? Here is why having an answer is so important. Being authentic simply means keeping it real. I know that can be challenging in the workplace. As organizations continue to focus on the importance of teamwork and collaboration, it is important that we as leaders are able to develop and sustain strong relationships at all levels within the organization.

Not only is it key to developing strong relationships, but it prevents you from attempting to please everyone. When you know who you are and are confident in yourself, you can be unapologetic and unswerving in striving to achieve your goals.

I had just completed my first year of college and was working as an intern at a large company. One day my manager asked me to bring in my college catalog so that we could review the courses required to complete my degree program. He determined that there were not enough computer programming courses in the computer engineering program and said that I needed to change my major to computer science.

However, I refused his suggestion. At that time in my life, I was very clear on the fact that I was going to earn my computer engineering degree. Period. I knew that I was not a programmer and had no desire to take additional programming classes since that did not fit into my big picture goals. I also knew that I did not want to return to Jacksonville, Florida upon graduating from college. There was this big world out there, and I wanted to explore it.

But what if I did not know who I am? What if I were not clear on who I was and what I wanted? I could have been talked into a role that I did not love merely because it sounded like a good idea. This was one of the first opportunities to stand my ground and stay on course to achieve my vision and not deviate because of someone else and their well-meaning intentions.

Think of a time that you did something that did not align with your passions. How did you feel? How well did you perform in that role?

When not being clear on who you are, you run the risk of being a people pleaser and/or pursuing roles that are not aligned with where you are supposed to go. There will be many opportunities to abandon the course because well-meaning people will encourage you to do something different and often their arguments are convincing.

As a leader, you must be willing to stand, even if alone, for your beliefs. Not everyone will see the vision when you do.

On Discovering Your Purpose

When you want to discover your purpose, some experts suggest looking back at your childhood. As I looked back at my childhood I wondered how I had gotten so far off track. As a child, I had an uncle who called me "radio," because I talked so much. From what I understand it was pretty much non-stop as long as I was awake. However, as I got older I became more quiet and reserved to the point that speaking seemed like the least likely thing for me to do.

My grandmother says that I have been teaching all of my life. As a little girl I would read books and then go to my room and teach my students, except there was no one else in the room. However, everyone had a name, and I made sure they received the information. During my undergraduate years, people would often ask me if I were an education major, and I would flippantly respond, "No, I have a real major. I'm an engineering major." Some even went so far as to say that I looked like a teacher.

What are some of those clues that you have been getting along the way that you have stubbornly ignored?

Honestly, I did not want to be a teacher, because teachers did not make enough money. I never even considered being a college professor, trainer, or other type of "teacher." I stubbornly stayed my course to pursue my engineering degree.

However, throughout my career I have trained others in some

capacity whether formally or informally. It is like it is part of my DNA in that I enjoy sharing information with others to help them become better. Fairly early in my career, I found myself working at a small college in Florida. Upon completing my masters degree, I found myself in the classroom, and to my surprise, I loved it!

Over the years following that, I often taught part-time as an adjunct instructor. To this day, I still teach some courses at times, and of course, training is such a big part of my business. What is that one thing in your heart that will not go away? Spend some quiet time reflecting on your childhood.

What were your natural inclinations at that time?
What did you enjoy doing?
What did you want to be?

Write your thoughts down in your journal. You may have to ask a parent or sibling to help you with this exercise. Ask them to tell you about your early childhood.

The Lies

I do not know about you, but I cannot stand a liar. I especially cannot stand when someone lies to another person about their potential and their abilities. How many of us have had parents, teachers, mentors, peers, or media speak negatively over our lives? They say things such as "you will never amount to anything" or "you are just like your no-good daddy."

Or what about lies such as, "women don't have what it takes to lead major corporations" or "in order to be successful you have to lead like a man"? How can I lead like a man when I am a woman? These statements are simply not true.

Research shows that a woman's use of more collaborative or

transformational leadership styles are more effective and work well in today's ever-changing workplace. Stop trying to employ the old paradigm of authoritarian leadership as the way to go, particularly if it does not align with your true style. You must be authentic in your leadership. Take the time to discover and develop your authentic leadership style.

The Power of "I Am"

Your words have power, and they have life. You can change your current condition by beginning with changing your words. Listen to your self-talk. What are you saying about yourself? Are you simply repeating the negative things that you have heard spoken about you in the past or are you saying things that lift you up?

If you want to change your world, you must change your words. Make a decision right now that you will speak positive words about you and your future. Acknowledge where you are and your role in how you got there, but know that you have the choice to do something different.

Peatric chose different. Her adult life began with the odds against her. Peatric was 18 years old when she graduated from high school and became pregnant. She married and began her life as a young wife and mother. Because of her decision, she was told that she would be relegated to living a life of poverty. But Peatric refused to speak those words over her life.

She was determined not to allow other people's opinions to stand in her way. Peatric entered nursing school at the age of 19. Years later, she joyfully balances the roles of home and work. Having completed a master's degree, Peatric excelled in her field and became a manager of case management and director of nursing. She and her husband worked hard and were able to purchase a home.

No matter what others may have said about you in the past, you can make the choice today to say something different. You can make the choice today to begin taking the actions necessary to move you in the direction of achieving your goal. Or you can make the choice to continue to believe what they have said and continue repeating it to yourself, thus continuing to create the environment or situation that you currently see.

Your Openness With Others

Growth in an organization depends on effective relationships. If you want to go higher or move around in your career, you need to have a network. People need to know and respect you. However, in order to build genuine relationships, you must be able to establish trust. How do you build trust when you are hiding behind a mask or you are not being real? How do you effectively lead a team when you do not know who you are?

Others can sense when you are being fake or phony. They may not be able to put their finger on it, but they know that something is not quite right. Von stated, "Sometimes being a manager was like being a mom. You had to be strong for the people that worked for you." However, during the rough periods when upper management was putting on pressure, Von felt she had to put up a front. Often others in the organization, whether they report to you or not, assume that you know more than you do simply because of your position within the organization. Yet, Von disclosed that was not the case. "So, often I knew so little. I knew just about as much as everybody that worked for me, but because of your role there's this assumption that you have all of this knowledge." She felt that sometimes she went too far in her front and people thought she was phony. Despite her uncertainty, Von felt that she had to hold it together emotionally, particularly during times of change. "It becomes a balancing act of staying calm and hold it together so that they aren't falling apart," she said.

Vulnerability

There is a quiet strength in being vulnerable. It is not always easy to admit our flaws, especially in the workplace. When I mention being vulnerable to leaders, many cringe and rightfully so. It is often quite risky to be vulnerable in organizations. However, I believe it is worth it and the higher up you go, the more important this becomes. To be vulnerable means to open up to the possibility of being hurt, criticized, or ridiculed for being who you are.

One of the biggest obstacles to authenticity is fear of rejection. What if I am who I am and then I am rejected? What happens then?

Honestly, I am not a fan of being vulnerable of putting myself at risk, and I know many others that feel the same way. However, in her research, Dr. Brené Brown posits that vulnerability is the key to being authentic and real. In her TED talk, she stated, "Connection is what gives meaning and purpose to our lives." As a leader, connecting to those you work with adds depth and quality to your relationships. It is difficult to build trust and credibility if you are hiding behind a wall afraid to be yourself."[29]

Creating an invisible wall will cause your team to hold back or put up walls of its own. This wall essentially creates a barrier to developing a genuine, authentic relationship. As a leader, you are to help others grow and develop their unique skills and talents. This becomes a challenge when there is a lack of relationship.

Brené states that it takes courage to be vulnerable whether at work or in your personal relationships. I loved the definition of courage that she used, which was "to tell the story of who you are with your whole heart." Where is the fear of being real holding you back in your relationships? What steps can you take today to be more real and authentic?

Facing Vulnerability

In all honesty, I did not want to share this story in this book. It felt far too personal and what if I am judged as a result of it? However, as a leader, I must walk the talk so here goes.

One evening after another sleepless and restless night, my concerned husband asked me if I was feeling OK. During our conversation, he asked the question, "Have you gained weight?" Initially, I became defensive, "Did he really just ask me that? He has never asked me that!"

I know my husband and his heart, and I knew he did not ask the question out of malice or ill-will. With all sincerity, He was trying to analyze the situation so that he could fix it, and I could sleep. But goodness ... did he have to ask me that question?

The truth was undeniable. Yes, I had gained weight, and it was quite noticeable, especially to me. My jeans felt more snug around my mid-section, and my hormones had been a raging mess. Despite my efforts of maintaining my eating regimen, it was not paying off when it came to those lovely three digits on that scale.

It had been one of those weeks where you walk by the scale

and give it the stank-eye while secretly wishing you could smash it to pieces. But my weight issues had a root problem that I did not want to admit was affecting me not only physically, but mentally.

Several years ago, I was diagnosed with polycystic ovarian syndrome or PCOS, which is an endocrine disorder where a woman's hormones are completely and utterly out of whack (Dr. Nadia's non-medical definition). Some of the symptoms are infertility, acne, and weight gain, especially around the middle. Doctors often shared the grim news that not only would it be difficult or impossible to get pregnant, it may also be difficult (or impossible) to lose weight! Why am I sharing this?

Because whether you want to admit it or not, the way you feel about yourself and your overall health impact your leadership performance at work. It is even more frustrating when you feel like you are doing everything right, and yet you are still not seeing the results you want to see.

As I write this book, I am focusing on getting back into the groove of business and working on my new project, but it has been stressful. Add in the fact that I am not feeling my best, and I do not feel that I look my best adding insult to injury.

It has been difficult to focus due to a lack of sleep. Because of my type-A personality, I tend to just say, "I need to work a little harder, or I just need to be more disciplined and it will get better." But none of that internal pep talk was improving my performance or helping me accomplish my goals.

That is where having a mentor or coach like my friend and coach, Angella Johnson, is helpful. As she and I were talking, Angella could tell by the sound of my voice and the deflection of my responses that something was not right. So instead of building up a wall by lying , "Nothing. Nothing is wrong. I am fine," I chose to kill that standard lie with the honest, vulnerable truth. I shared with Angella what was happening in my life.

Vulnerability is not an easy thing to do. But when shared with a trustworthy person, it can be the lifesaver to keep you from drowning.

Angella's response to my story was, "Be easy on yourself." Whew! Relief. It was not a "get out of jail free" card, which meant I no longer had to work hard and handle my business, but it was permission to admit that there are some things that are out of my control. It was permission to acknowledge that I will not have all of the answers. It was permission to recognize that when I am physically, emotionally, and hormonally off, it affects every single area of my life whether I like it or not.

Sometimes your support team is not there to help you do anything except to remind you to give yourself a break. Everything is not going to be perfect, and there are some things that are beyond your immediate control.

After our conversation, she forwarded me the contact information of someone who could relate to what I was going through in case I wanted to talk about it more. Not only could she relate, but she shared the findings of her personal research along with her story.

While reading the contact's story detailing her journey with PCOS, her findings and her approach, I began to not only feel better, but I began to see that I had options. You see, I still had a choice to make. Was I going to sit there and whine about it or was I going to do something?

Three years ago when I decided to make some serious changes in my health, it paid off big. Not only did I lose weight and feel great, but I was able to stop taking asthma and allergy medications after 20 years! It was nothing short of miraculous. So surely, if I just stayed the course it would help with this too, right? Maybe not.

The process just did not fit my life and my new hectic schedule. It no longer served me, and now, I may have to find another way. In reading her story and her research, I found an option that not only fit my lifestyle, but also fit my desire to take a more holistic approach to my health.

I could make the choice to continue doing things the way that I have been or I could try something new. By making minor shifts in my daily routine and actions, I could have a major impact on my mood, my health, and my waistline.

What is going on in your world right now? Is there a trustworthy person in your network with whom you can be vulnerable? The definition for insanity is doing the same thing and expecting a different result. Drop the mask and be more authentic.

Instead of beating yourself up about a problem or trying to solve it yourself, why not open up and see if there might be a better way? Be easy on yourself.

Reach for the Sky

Where there is no vision, the people perish.
Proverbs 29:18

What do you want? Where do you want to go? What is that dream position that you have been eyeing for a long time? Do you want to have a corner office, to become a CEO, or to start a non-profit?

In working with clients, one of the first things we work on is becoming crystal clear on the big vision. What does she want to accomplish in the next 12-18 months? What does she want within the next 3-5 years? If you do not know where you are going, how will you know when you get there?

Having a vision for your career is crucial for your career success. Your vision is a detailed description of where you want to go, and you have to write it down.

Writing out your vision or creating a vision board of some sort helps to make it real. You should review your vision and goals daily. Keep them before you so that as you make decisions, you are sure that they are aligned with your final destination.

Not only does writing the vision make it more real, but it also helps to keep your mind focused. Having a clear vision of your goals will eliminate distractions, because you are targeting the bigger picture. Another great thing about having a written vision is that it will help you to determine which opportunities are best and which ones are only good. It makes the not-so-exciting parts of your journey more bearable.

When I was working on my dissertation, I recall encountering two young ladies who we will call *Peggy and *Tracy. Both were young female professionals of the same age working for a large financial institution. Neither of them were particularly happy in their role, but they strived to make the best of their situations. While working at this institution, there were often complaints of unfair treatment, lower wages, favoritism, and career stagnation.

In the midst of an unfavorable working environment, Peggy and Tracy had a decision to make. I can either stay where I am and tough it out, or I can do what it takes to make things better for me. Each lady chose a different path than the other. Tracy decided that it was not necessarily the company that was all bad, but the department in which she worked that needed to make a shift. Tracy set a goal to leave the department and relocate to another city. She took the time to build her network in another city, completed online classes to improve her skill set, and applied for other roles. Within several months, she had landed a job in her goal city and continued to build her career.

During Tracy's transition when unfavorable and unwanted situations reared their ugly heads, she did not get discouraged, because she knew that those circumstances were only temporary. She turned her frustration into motivational fuel that would propel her to the next step in her career. Tracy confidently knew that the tactical skills and knowledge that she gained in her role would only help her in her next leadership position.

Meanwhile, Peggy chose to do the opposite of Tracy's actions. Peggy remained in the same position and department. She had no vision for where she wanted to go or what she wanted to do. Sadly, Peggy had resigned herself to the relative discomfort of completing her career in the glass cage. In a casual conversation with Peggy, I asked her if she could imagine seeing herself sitting at the same desk doing the same job for the next 30 plus years. Peggy did not give me a response, but her silence and inaction spoke volumes: "This was as good as it was going to get." Peggy who was only in her early 30s failed to cultivate a vision to direct her life. At the time of this writing, which is five years after that casual conversation, Peggy is still working in that same role.

A Colorful Vision

At the age 17, I promised my grandmother Dorothy that I would "get all of the colors." I was preparing to graduate from high school and head off to college. I was so excited, but could not decide on which college I wanted to attend. Education was a big deal in my family, particularly for my grandparents.

My grandparents grew up at a time when education for blacks was not acceptable by mainstream society. My grandmother had a third grade education and my grandfather was illiterate. Their lack of formal education ignited a deep passion within them to have all of their children and grandchildren attend school and get "their lesson."

For the first seven years of my life, I lived with them, and they were instrumental in developing my passion for learning and reading. My enjoyment of school was evident, so it was no surprise to them that I went on to college. I often joke and say that I had no choice. I had a bachelor's degree in my sights, but prior to a life-changing conversation with my granny, I had not made plans to earn a doctoral degree.

Sitting and listening to my granny always brought peace to my heart. On this pivotal day, she told me about attending my cousin's doctoral commencement ceremony. My grandmother re-envisioned all the doctoral graduates seated before the platform. "I remember all of the colors," My granny said. As she described what she saw I imagined how beautiful and special that display must have been. When finished painting this colorful picture of achievement, she turned to me and said, "Promise that you too will get all of the colors." And I agreed.

Fast forward many years later to me sitting at the commencement ceremony for my master's degree. The speaker that day described the essence of the doctoral robe. He talked about the honor of wearing the gown with the velvet stripes and the tam that only doctoral candidates wear. It was an unforgettable, beautiful picture. Then, I remembered. The speaker's words drew me back to my granny's promise. After the graduation ceremony, I was walking to the car with my mom. I turned to her and said, "I have to go back and get my velvet robe."

Less than a year after I completed my masters, I began my doctoral journey. It was not easy completing that degree, and I had many opportunities to quit. One of the things that kept me going was the opportunity to tell my granny that I had finally gotten all of the colors. I would daydream about what I would say in my acknowledgements section or what I would say at my graduation party. Keeping that image before me helped me to not throw in the towel when roadblocks or obstacles came up. Even when people attempted to discourage me from pursuing that route I stayed the course. Are you that committed to achieving your dream? Think of a vivid, colorful image that will keep you pressing forward when you feel like quitting. Bring that picture to mind on a regular basis and watch it come to life.

Vision Pouters and Doubters

Despite your personal excitement about the vision for your career, close friends and family might not share in your enthusiasm. Instead of hearing "congratulations", you could encounter their concerned whispers. At that point, you have to choose to stick with your vision or comply with the wishes of your loved ones.

When I completed my undergraduate degree, I was offered a job with IBM in Dallas, Texas. I was so excited. Texas was one of the places on my list of places to live and here was the perfect opportunity to do it. The best part about the job offer was that it was given six months before graduation. This meant I could complete my degree without the stress and pressure of having to find a job. However, when I called my mom to share the great news, she was less than thrilled.

I remember so clearly.

Me: "Mom, I have great news I got a job offer."

Mom: "Really, where?"

Me: I was offered a job with IBM in Dallas!

Mom: Silence.

That was not good. I know my mom. When she gets silent like that, it means she is not pleased. I understood that she was concerned. I, her firstborn, unmarried daughter, had only been three hours away by car. But now, I would be two and a half hours away by plane! Despite my mom's initial disappointment, I did not let it sway me. I went for it and you know what? She eventually came around.

She had six months before I graduated college to get comfortable with the idea of me moving to Dallas versus returning to Jacksonville. By the time graduation day rolled around she joined in my excitement about my move and the next chapter in my life. Sometimes those closest to us do not see our vision right away and that is OK. Stay steady and move forward.

As a leader, your role is to see the vision and clearly communicate the vision. However, you must be willing to stand alone when people do not accept your vision. If you abandon the vision at the first sign of a disagreement, you will never go anywhere.

Be cautious of allowing others to talk you out of what you know is true. Be mindful: They could mean well, but it does not mean that they are right. It can be challenging to remain committed and motivated to your big vision when others do not see it and do not support it.

Keep in mind that loved ones also might be the cheerleaders of your vision. Peatric was able to find support and discipline from the women in her family to help her fulfill her vision. In turn, it empowered Peatric to be that same woman for her daughters and other young women seeking a mentor.

"As women we all have different motivators," Peatric said. She wanted to be a role model for her daughters so that they could see a real-life, tangible example of a woman leader. Peatric wanted that person to be her versus looking at a woman in the media.

In addition, there were three women who influenced her greatly as she developed the vision for her future. These women were her mother, grandmother, and aunt. "My grandmother was a very hard worker. If she earned a dollar she saved a quarter." Peatric adopted her grandmother's work ethic and how she handled money.

As a child, Peatric grew up poor and watched how her mom made things work with limited resources. From this, she saw how to manage when things were tight and how to not be paralyzed by material lack. This also helped shape Peatric's vision for the future, because she knew that she did not want to always live this way.

Peatric's aunt helped to shape Peatric's vision. "I learned from my aunt the type of life I wanted to live. I looked at her, and she drove a Camaro [and] had a cute apartment with cute furniture, and I thought, 'Oh my gosh, look at how she lives.'" Peatric knew that it was going to take hard work, determination, proper money management, and a strong will to not allow her present circumstances to distract her from her vision. Having the example of her aunt's life clearly showed that there was more to life than what she knew. Plus, if her aunt could do it, she could, too. If you are going to shatter your inner glass ceiling, you must have the same tenacity and commitment to your vision with or without family support.

Identify and Fortify Your Strengths

"You cannot be anything you want to be, but you can be a lot more of who you are already"
Tom Rath

When I speak to women and we talk about their strengths and desires, the conversation generally begins with them identifying their weaknesses and the things they would like to change about themselves. Unfortunately, the sad reality is that we are often trained and socialized to focus on improving our areas of weakness. How often in your performance is the majority of the discussion focused on what was done well? How often as a leader is your focus on finding what your team members can do better?

According to Marcus Buckingham, author of *First, Break All the Rules*, 81 percent of the workforce is more focused on improving their weaknesses than their strengths.[30] Additionally, 59 percent of the workforce believes they will be more successful if they can improve their weaknesses versus taking advantage of their strengths. However, research in Tom Rath's book *Strengths Finder 2.0* shows that when people focus on their strengths instead of their weaknesses, they are "six times as likely to be engaged in their jobs and more than three times as likely to report having an excellent quality of life in general."[31]

There is an adage: What we focus on grows. Yet, how often do we really embrace what that means? When we continue to focus on our weaknesses, it diminishes our strengths. Weaknesses do not empower us to operate at our highest level of performance.

In my undergraduate years studying computer engineering, I often found myself in challenging classes. By the time I completed my degree, I realized that there were many aspects of this profession that I not only did not like, but were not my strengths. One such area was computer programming. I was clear enough upon graduating to never apply for a position for programming; however, I spent many years in a field where I was not living up to my strengths.

Because I excelled throughout my corporate career, I did not really pay attention to how focusing on my weakness was truly impacting me. However, once I started my own company I became more aware of the power of focusing on my strengths. While it is important to know the ins and outs of your business, when I brought in team members who excelled in areas where I did not my business began to grow by leaps and bounds.

No longer did I spend hours doing tasks that were not my core strengths and slowing down my progress. Each person on my team is strong in their area of expertise, and they love what they do. What seemed like a chore to me is a delight for them. It is a win-win and as the leader, I respect their talents and allow them room to do what they do best.

Julie Gleeson and Sherry Platt Berman, cite a study by the National Science Foundation, in their book *Inside Job* that shows that up to 50,000 thoughts run through our heads every day.[32] Unfortunately, for many of us those thoughts are negative. I recently spoke with *Alice, a very accomplished professional woman. She was working on a bachelor's degree and had overcome many obstacles to achieve her level of career success, but she felt that she always focused on the negative. Alice was tired of trying to fix that one thing that was seemingly wrong and tired of trying to be perfect.

One thing in particular that plagued Alice was her feeling that she should say more during meetings. She said that the ideas do not flow until she leaves brainstorming meetings. If she has time to prepare then she is a creative contributor, but thinking on the fly was not her strength. Alice was overly focused on coming up with witty ideas on a whim during meetings that she overlooked all of the other great things that she did in her job and in her career, such as writing and planning. She took the initiative to focus on her strengths and develop them to improve her performance. Alice discovered that if she took a moment to jot her ideas on a sticky note prior to sharing them with the group she was able to share better. I worked with Alice to get over the hurdle of brainstorming meetings by taking a different approach and working to her strength. She is one that needs to think things through and see it in writing prior to verbalizing the idea. By changing her focus she was able to see her strength in being creative versus focusing on her weakness of not feeling that she was able to think quickly on her feet.

As we continued to talk, Alice shared how her mind was

consumed with negative thoughts and that she would verbalize these things to herself on how she was not good at one thing or another. I told her that she was being way too hard on herself, and she admitted that she was her own worst critic. I shared with her that she was not alone.

For women, identifying strengths is often a challenge. According to Marcus Buckingham, women are more likely to attribute their success to external factors, such as their team, whereas men are more likely to attribute their success to internal factors such as their own strengths, skills, or abilities.[33]

As women, we simply underestimate our talents and value. We do not consider our strengths as being strengths. First, take this challenge: Think about what you are thinking about. Take the time to journal the thoughts that pop into your head throughout the day. Are they positive or negative? Are they true or false? How can you turn a negative thought into a positive statement that you can repeat aloud?

One of the challenges in today's corporate environment is the focus on areas of improvement and employee flaws. This hypersensitivity on improvement and areas of perceived weakness increases the level of criticism and negativity in the workplace. What if we were to change our focus to how to best utilize and develop our strengths and the strengths of those around us? How do you determine your strengths?

One of my favorite strengths assessments is the *Strengths Finder 2.0* by Tom Rath. This assessment provides a comprehensive look at your strengths and those of your team members. One thing that I found after taking this assessment is that it highlights traits that you may not have considered strengths. We often underestimate our gifts and talents simply because it is easy to us. How can my gift of being able to work a room possibly be a gift?

Grab a journal and answer the following questions:

- **What are your gifts and talents?**
- **What is that one thing that you love to do and you lose all track of time?**
- **What are the things that come most natural to you?**
- **Why do you like doing these things?**
- **What draws you to these activities?**

Once you have identified your strengths brainstorm ways that you can utilize your strengths in your everyday work. The one way to continue to build upon your strengths is to continually use them and fortify them. Seek opportunities or ways to stretch yourself and grow your skills. Do not simply rely on doing this at work. What are some other ways to develop your strengths? Are there networking groups or other volunteer opportunities that will afford you the opportunity to develop your strengths? Be creative when considering your options.

Isha, founder of Epiphany Institute, shared the story of her time at Dow. She shared that she came to a point when she looked around the company and did not see anyone that she wanted to be like. Therefore, she took time to consider how she could have a role doing something that she enjoyed doing while making a significant impact.

Isha took an inventory of her skills and talents only to find that they did not align with a significant need in the company. This is when she decided to create her own role. However, during this time the company was in the midst of making substantial investments in a video infrastructure in order to build out the company's brand.

This is when Isha looked at her skills inventory and noted that she had a background in broadcast journalism and understood ways to use this new medium strategically to communicate with employees, customers, and other stakeholders. So she developed a job description and outlined how her skills and talents that could help the company make the most effective use of this new technology and infrastructure.

"When I first created the role, I thought it was going to get shot down," Isha said. However, she did not allow the fear to stop her and she moved forward with her proposal. As a result of this, her proposal was accepted and Isha received her newly created job. She shared that because her proposal focused on the value to the company and the return on their investment, it was an easy decision for her leadership.

Being mindful of your strengths will work wonders for you. When I decided that it was time for me to pursue my dream of having my own business where I would train and develop other women leaders, I was scared out of my mind. I had a long list of reasons why I was not yet qualified to do it. I seemed to forget my years of industry and teaching experience along with the three degrees I had managed to earn along the way. It was reflecting on my strengths that helped me push out of negativity and into action.

One of my greatest strengths is teaching. My granny often tells stories about me as a little girl teaching anyone and anything that would sit still and listen. As I mentioned previously, throughout my undergraduate years, people would often ask me if I were an education major. Apparently, they thought I looked like a teacher. No matter what role I held within a company, training or teaching others would become a component of my role in some way.

When I completed my master's degree, I was working at a college and found myself in the classroom. Ever since that time, I would teach courses on a part-time basis. However, I did not consider speaking to be my strength. I honestly never equated teaching and speaking so the thought of being a speaker frightened me even though I have often had to speak and present in front of people. Yet, after I looked at it in a different way, and I took a chance on trying it, I found that not only did I love it, but it is one of my strengths and a core piece of what I do.

Another personal attribute that I did not consider a strength is what Tom Rath called futuristic. After completing the *Strengths Finder 2.0* assessment, I found it interesting that this one was in my top five. According to Rath people who are futuristic are dreamers who see the vision of what could be. I am generally not fazed just because it has not been done before. Yet, in my experience it was often frowned upon to focus on the future. I was often encouraged to focus on the present.

However, as I learned more about this strength, I was excited. As a leader, being a visionary is key and can help inspire others to work toward more. Tom Rath states that someone who is futuristic "might excel in entrepreneurial or start-up situations."[34] That would explain why the roles where I had the most fun during my corporate career were often when the team was trying something new.

What are some of the things that you do well, yet you do not consider them strengths? It is important for you to believe in your own value. As they say during the safety instructions on a flight, you must put your oxygen mask on first before helping others. If you have a negative or poor self-image, chances are you judge everyone else through that lens, which means you have a negative perception of them as well. If you are focused only on team members' weaknesses, trust me you will find them and you will lose the opportunity to be an effective leader toward your team.

Helping Others See the Value in Themselves

As a leader, you must also be able to help others see and enhance their strengths. In my workshops, I sometimes put on big sunglasses to demonstrate the need to have big vision. One of the components toward encouraging vision is communicating it to others. Team members inherently want to do well, but they often underestimate their value and contribution to the big vision. Therefore, not only is it important to communicate the vision, but you must also help each individual team member see how what they do every day carries that vision forward.

Focusing on strengths does not mean to overlook what may need to improve, but it does mean that you are not solely focused on catching people (including yourself) doing things wrong. When there are opportunities to improve, you can use those as coaching moments to help improve team member performance and maintain employee engagement.

Some experts estimate that approximately 65 percent of U.S. employees are unhappy in their jobs and many blame their boss. It is estimated that it is costing organizations $360 billion per year in lost productivity.[35] Additionally, according to human resource magazines, employees do not leave organizations, they leave their managers. According to Jim Giuliano, despite the poor economy and massive layoffs, people still cite "ineffective leadership" or "poor relationship with their boss" as top reasons why they left an organization.[36] Therefore, it behooves you and your organization to take the time to assess your strengths and discover how to best utilize the strengths in your team members.

Design Your Success Blueprint

Once you have identified who you are, what you want, and what are your fabulous gifts and talents, it is now time to develop the blueprint or road map of how you are going to fulfill your vision.

Now, that you have outlined your vision and identified your strengths, it is time to pull it all together into a plan of action. Simply daydreaming about what you would like to achieve with no plan is a guaranteed way not to achieve your goals. Having a vision alone is simply not enough. You must have a plan.

Most people spend more time planning vacations or checking emails than they do planning their careers. According to Thomas Denham, "most people spend more time planning [their] vacation than they do planning their careers."[37] How much time have you spent developing a success plan for your career?

If you are going to excel in your career and shatter the inner glass ceiling, you must have a written plan. Developing your roadmap by creating a career portfolio is essential. The first action step is to know career expectations and then exceed them.

Exceed Performance Expectations

There is no way to get around performance. Ascending to the upper ranks of an organization or starting your own enterprise will take hard work and dedication. Having a lackluster attitude towards performance will not work.

In order to excel in the ranks and gain respect you must be good at what you do. Peatric recommends that women remain current on industry trends and become a guru in something. Commit right now to becoming a lifelong learner. It does not always have to mean a formal degree, but take the initiative to acquire new skills and information on your own time. Do not solely rely on your company to do it all and provide you with all the training that you may need. If you work for a company that has a large learning and development department that offers free skills training, then by all means take advantage of it. However, if not, what can you do to obtain the skills that you need?

Barbara shared that a key to her success was her commitment to excellence. "Anything less than excellence [wasn't] an option," She said. She also stressed the importance of preparation. "Always be prepared for an opportunity that does not yet exist," Barbara quoted as her motto.

Your goal should be to become recognized as an expert or leader in your field. Refuse to rest on your laurels. Constantly focus on learning by reading magazines or trade magazines and taking classes. After evaluating your skills, develop a plan to address any skill gaps that you may have identified. Work towards filling those gaps and then keep your skills fresh and updated. Seek opportunities to take on high profile assignments or to take on additional responsibilities to gain skills that are outside your area of expertise.

Connie shared that despite not having a bachelor's degree, being a constant learner even outside of her area of expertise paid off big dividends in her career,. Connie took the initiative to learn new skills on her own time through professional organizations. As a member of Minority Interchange (MI), she learned skills, such as Lotus application software. Then, back at her workplace, Connie would ask to back up someone on her team or try a new assignment using the new knowledge she acquired. If management gave her push back because they thought she did not have the training, she would tell them that in fact she did have the training. Connie's involvement with MI gave her the confidence she needed to continue to pursue more advanced positions. "As a result of that I was able to build relationships, learn things, get training, and gain exposure out of this world," she said.

Another method for lifelong learning is through certification. Von stated, "Keep learning. If you have an opportunity to be educated inside your company or externally [and get] a certification, take it. That's important, too, because it broadens you and you really do not know what the next opportunity is going to be. Most careers are not a straight path to the CEO. There are zigzags, and there are other kinds of things. Maybe you're the woman who is going to start her own company. It's not a path that I chose, but it certainly is possible."

When Dow needed on-camera video talent to launch a global awareness campaign it sent out a call for audition tapes. Isha recalls that the team reviewing the tapes did not find what they needed.

That is when Isha remembered that she had done a television spot for the company in a different state, however no one on her team was aware of it. "I had two options. I could be quiet about it or I could speak up and let them know about my experience," Isha said. So she decided to share with them her experience and offered to participate in the video. She brought in tapes and other information to demonstrate what she had done in the past.

Needless to say, Isha received the position. "That was the most fun I had in the nine years that I was there," Isha said. As a result of this new role, Isha had the opportunity to do a live broadcast from the United Nations with Hilary Swank. "[That] put me on the map where employees around the world knew who I was," Isha shared. Lifelong learning along with tooting her own horn gave Isha the confidence to put an action plan to her vision. Not only that, but it thrust her into the presence of others. The next action step is to increase your executive presence.

Increase Your Executive Presence

You must be visible. Although hard work and great performance are required, they alone are not enough. Decision makers within the organization should know who you are, what your capabilities are, and where you want to go. Whether you think it is fair or not, informal networking is a key component to career growth and should be a part of your success strategy. Who are the movers and shakers within your organization? How can you get on their calendars to schedule a brief chat or have a coffee meeting?

Connie knows the value of increasing executive presence. She received a promotion because of it. Connie was assigned as the team leader of training over a continuous quality improvement process project (a project designed to encourage people to share their ideas and put them on the table). Connie said that as the project lead her job was to take the supervisors and turn them into team leads. Her senior management team thought it would be easy. But Connie was met face first with challenges.

"I had to come up with the process to help people make the transition from supervisor to team lead and what that means," Connie said. The managers, however, did not understand how to make the shift. "So how do you get your supervisors to understand it when they report to these managers who are still asking for the same things and treating them the same way? So, how do you make that happen?" What could have been perceived as a major roadblock became a great opportunity for Connie to showcase her creativity. This meant Connie had to come up with a creative way to address the need for a cultural shift if the new process was going to work. Connie relied on her learning training through MI and came up with the idea to have a show called "The O-Pru Winning show" based on a worldwide famous talk show.

The idea was organized and treated as if it were an actual TV show. "We had our marketing department do commercials," Connie said. The talk included guests, executives who showed up as the personalities of famous celebrities and well-known persons, such as Dr. Ruth, Dr. Joyce, and John Wayne . Additionally, the audience was live. Connie organized "plants" in the audience to cue up certain topic discussions. "We did all these analogies," Connie explained. "We actually laid out all these serious issues in this fun format and addressed them."

Connie bravely included senior-level executives in her talk show idea, and as a result, they were fully engaged in the process. The senior vice president was so impressed that he said to her, "Where did you get these skills? Please don't quit because you could do this for a living." She received numerous accolades and two weeks later, she was promoted. This happened despite being told earlier that another promotion that she was being considered for might be delayed.

While on the topic of executive presence, I want you to think about how you look—your appearance. As much as we would like to say and believe that looks have nothing to do with our career advancement, the reality is that it does matter. I was taught early on to dress for the position you want, not the one you have. Also, the way you dress impacts your confidence. So as you take the actions necessary to shatter the glass ceiling, you must look and feel fabulous doing so. Can you imagine Connie showing up to her talk show idea wearing drab and dull attire? Part of her dress, which is fabulous, played a part in getting her positive recognition from the executives.

In the words of Zig Ziglar, "When your image improves, your performance improves." Take a look at how you show up to work. Does your attire look like how the executives are dressing? How is your hair or makeup? If this is not your area of expertise, then get a friend or hire an image consultant to help you out. The truth is the better you look, the more confident you feel. People also take you more seriously when you dress and carry yourself in a certain manner versus wearing a wardrobe that does not emote engagement and interest. This leads to the next action plan step: Once you up your presence, get around others who are on board to support you.

Build Your Support Team

Earlier we discussed the importance of networking. When constructing your success blueprint, a key piece of that is the persons you select for your support team. You must identify resourceful people within your organization and outside of your organization who can speak on your behalf and inform you of available positions. Oftentimes, these contacts can inform you of positions that are on the horizon and are not yet public knowledge. Ultimately, this provides you with a favorable competitive advantage.

Peatric stresses that networking is very important. "I didn't do enough networking, and I feel that it would have helped me obtain new roles a lot quicker. You have to develop those relationships," Peatric urged.

Informal relationships and connections are imperative to advancing your career. Research shows that as many as 80 percent of jobs are not advertised.[38] I know from personal experience of the impact of having a "Team Nadia." I have enjoyed the privilege of interviewing for unadvertised positions and even "applying" for a job that I knew was already mine even though for formality sake it appeared on the company's Intranet.

This happened because people knew who I was and that I excelled in my job performance. My team was aware of where I wanted to go so when the job opportunity was still in the idea phase, I was the person they already had in mind to call. How would you like to receive that call with a job offer and all you have to do is say yes? OK, I had to do more than just say yes, but it was pretty close.

When it comes to building your support team, you must be strategic. Mirella Visser states in her book that you must connect with people who have "a say in the organization [who] have a positive opinion about your capabilities and are willing to support you."[39] Who are some of the people within and outside of your organization that you can connect with and begin to build relationships? Remember that it takes time to build strong relationships. Start now so you are not stranded if you find yourself in need. The final action plan step is to take calculated risks.

Take Calculated Risks

You cannot shatter the inner glass ceiling if you never take a risk. Given the current state of the economy and the challenges that many companies face, it is very tempting to simply play it safe. Why rock the boat if it is not necessary? Colleagues and friends will probably question why you would want to mess up a good thing. But if it were so good, you would not desire more. It does not mean that where you are is a bad place, it just means that it is time to try something different.

Ginni Rometty wisely said, "Comfort and growth do not coexist." If you are comfortable in your role and you can do it with your eyes closed, then you are not growing. In order to advance your career, you must continue to seek assignments and positions that stretch and challenge you.

This is how I have approached my career. I get bored easily, so I require constant challenges. I sometimes wish this were not the case, but it is the truth. That was one reason why I liked project management so much. Almost every day was an adventure! So it was no surprise that when I heard my company was doing some expanding, it piqued my interest. Although my initial goal was to move to Charlotte, North Carolina, I could not help but to inquire about what was going on out West.

Phoenix Bound

One day I received a call from a peer, and she asked if I might be interested in taking a position in Phoenix, Arizona. I told her that I was definitely interested in learning more so she asked me to send my resume to her manager, and we scheduled an interview.

This position was scary. It was definitely a stretch position for me, and I could not be happier. I knew I could do the role, but I had so much new stuff to learn before I would be truly proficient. I was offered the job, and I accepted.

Within three weeks I was on a plane headed to Los Angeles, California for training. In this role, I was thrust into what felt like an entirely new world. I was having a blast with learning, traveling, and networking. Then four months after beginning my new job, it all came to a screeching halt. My company was acquired by another company, and now my dream position was in jeopardy. For almost four agonizing months, I waited to see if my role would survive the cuts, and then I received the news that my position was being eliminated.

Wow! Really? Although I was not devastated, I was disappointed. However, after we received the news one of my peers asked me if I regretted my decision to accept the position and move. My answer was a resounding, "No!"

Despite how things looked, I knew that I would be OK. I immediately reached out to my network and started planning. My team was given a heads up before our official termination date, but there was no more guessing. We could start taking the action that we needed in order to secure our next position. I gained invaluable experience and made great connections when I moved. Although, things were not going according to my plan, it did not mean it was not a good move.

You see, almost two months after I left Florida, half of my team was let go including my manager. If I had remained, it was possible that I could have been one of those who were affected. Though taking the risk to accept the position and move to Phoenix did not prevent me from facing the same fate, no one knows what would have happened if I had remained. In the end, I was offered a position with a new company, and when I left, I departed on my own terms. Although it looked a little bleak for a moment, I never would have had the wonderful opportunities that I had if I had not been willing to take the risk.

"It is important to take risks, which prevents stagnation, helps you grow, and creates exposure," Barbara encouraged. In order to achieve the level of success in her career, Barbara purposefully took strategic, calculated risks. Some items on her risk resume include selecting a mentor, separating from a mentor, applying for more challenging roles, being open to relocation, and moving to a new city and state. Barbara also did not wait for permission, and she took the initiative to create new processes when there was a need. Naturally, Barbara also was willing to go against the norm and say no whenever warranted.

Connie shared that when it came to risks, she was not very smart. She admits that there were times when she was "suicidal when it came to [her] career." Career suicide is making decisions that may hinder your progress or chances of getting a promotion. With a laugh, Connie shared that she did not realize at the time that she was taking those types of careless risks. Connie shared that as a leader, she knew there "wasn't a whole lot [she] wasn't willing to do when it came to [her] people." Even if it meant losing her job, she would protect the people on her team. Connie survived her miscalculated risks and was winning and moving forward in her career in spite of those risky decisions.

Despite Connie's career success, she does not advise others to commit career suicide. While it is important to take risks, you do not want to take careless risks that will prevent your forward progress. Exceptions to this are when your values or morals are being challenged.

Questions to answer when assessing risk:

- **What am I risking if I do this? Is it worth it?**
- **What is the likelihood of things going my way?**
- **Is there a contingency? What will I do if things do not go my way?**
- **Am I willing to commit to the process and see it all the way through?**
- **Is now the right time?**

Making the decision to take a risk is a personal decision and must be assessed on an individual basis. Before taking a risk it is wise to do an honest assessment. You must be brutally honest with yourself and where you are in this season of your life and your career.

When looking at risk, it is dangerous to play the self-comparison game. You must be true to yourself and do what is right for you and your team. Barbara shared that learning to put things in perspective was essential when assessing risks. She stated that "being true to [herself] as a person, a woman, and a leader helped guide the risks [she] would take."

Barbara went on to share that because of her foundation and perspective on taking risks, "It wasn't so much about which risks to take as it was about when and how." Remember that timing is very important. "Timing along with the way you take the risks [are] very crucial components," Barbara added.

Execute Your Success Plan

A plan without action is useless! We have laid out the vision and road map, but the implementation can be a challenge. So often, clients get stuck—literally. I have found that taking action is a major fear buster. Dale Carnegie said, "Inaction breeds doubt and fear. But action breeds confidence and courage." In order to conquer fear, you must take action and do so in spite of your feelings. The good news is that feelings can and will change. Once you face your fear, you will be surprised at how good you feel.

What if you were to implement your career plan and pursue the position that you truly wanted? What if you were to have that challenging conversation with a team member? What if none of the things that you thought would happen, happened at all? Are you willing to take that chance?

I implore you to not take yourself out of the game before you even get started. Do not allow a fear of looking stupid or what people may say or even of making a mistake stop you. I have a news flash: You are going to make mistakes! I repeat: You are going to make mistakes! It is a part of life, and it is a part of the journey for a leader. Whenever you make a mistake, you get up, dust yourself off, learn from it, and move on.

It is going to feel awkward, but do it anyway. People are going to say no, but do it anyway. People may even talk about you, but do it anyway. Remember that a no today may be a yes tomorrow, but you will never know if you do not ask!

I remember a time when I applied for a project manager role within my firm. That new position appealed to my career interests. I went through the process and was not selected for the job. However, something very interesting happened. My leadership said to me, "Nadia we weren't aware that you were interested in doing more project management work." After I had put myself out there, my "no" became an opportunity for me to grow and learn from the person that was hired. My managers not only assigned me more projects, but higher profile projects that afforded me the opportunity to learn and get additional exposure to others in the organization.

Taking the chance that you might be turned away may work out for you even if it does not look the way you would like for it to look. While on the subject of asking, do not be afraid to ask for help. As a leader, you will never know it all. So continue to be open to learning and developing your skills. The pastor of my local church said, "You teach what you know, but you reproduce who you are." You cannot continue to grow and develop your team if you become stagnant in your own growth.

Not Pursuing Your Dream

You have to get comfortable with being uncomfortable in order to pursue your dream. I shared this with a good friend as we mused about someone we knew who was not pursuing his dream. However, not long after sharing this I had the opportunity to learn this lesson firsthand.

"You should start your own business." I lost count of how many times I heard those words or a similar variation of them. However, I was resistant to the idea. I was going to climb the corporate ladder, because starting a business seemed like a crazy and difficult risk. There is some comfort in knowing that every two weeks there is a check and that you have medical and dental insurance along with a retirement fund. As an entrepreneur, there are more unknowns, and it sometimes not only feels risky, but downright foolish to leave what you have to venture out and do something on your own. It was simply easier to do what was familiar.

Although I had this dream stirring in my heart, I continued to pursue the easier path. I would fight to find that "perfect" job where I would not get bored. I remember years ago asking my now husband, why could I not go to work and be happy. Why did I always have to want more? What was wrong with me?

Perhaps people have told you that your dream to achieve higher is too much.. Are you nagged by the question, why not just be happy with all that you have right now? Ignore them. Ignore their question. Do not allow them to make you feel guilty for not choosing to hide your light. Frankly, their desire to have you not move forward has nothing to do with you and everything to do with them. If you move forward with what is in your heart, it causes them to reflect on the fact that they are not pursuing their desires. They have allowed the lies, the disappointment, or the fear to convince them that it is better to stay where they are. But you have shattered your inner glass ceiling and now are unstoppable.

When Enough is Enough

Again. Another car ride home with tears in my eyes. The stinging words of my manager were on repeat in my mind. After another disastrous one-on-one with my manager, I was at the breaking point. When I spoke to Toby, I told him I did not want to go back. Because I am not a big crier, I think Toby actually considered that as a viable option in the moment. However, on Monday I went back to work.

In my entire career, I do not think I had ever felt so horrible. I do not think I had ever felt so frustrated, betrayed, and alone. Although this day was horrible, I knew long before this day that I was done with being stuck and done with being afraid. However, I kept trying to hang in there and pretend as if everything was OK. Honestly, it was scary to think about walking away from my career ladder and starting my entrepreneurial dream.

You see this was not the first time a manager and I did not see eye-to-eye. It also was not the first time that I had been stabbed in the back. In times past, I would have fought back with every ounce of my being. But this time I was done. I did not have it in me to fight for a position that I knew in my heart I did not want. I could no longer ignore the fact that it was time for me to move forward.

My clients have similar breaking points. *Cierra, a 36-year old accountant I coached, had been in her current role for more than five years and was fed up with dealing with their shenanigans.

She shared, "Nadia, I've had enough! I was so mad until

I was bawling!" Boy, could I relate. Some of her challenges included working long hours with little to no time off and lack of management support, because "the work wasn't suffering." Although the work was not suffering, the team surely was. Does any of this sound familiar to you?

During our session, we got to the root of her problem. Although, she knew that it was time to move out of her current position, fear had paralyzed her. Then, together we devised a plan for moving past that fear. After our call, not only did she have clear action steps, but she also had a new perspective and a new attitude.

Maybe your situation is different. As for me, I knew that it was time to branch out on my own and launch my business. Maybe for you it is time to move to a different department, or it is possibly time to work with an entirely different organization. No matter the underlying reason, the fact remains the same: It is painful to not pursue your dream.

The Power of a Decision

Once you make up your mind to do something, it is amazing how things suddenly begin to fall into place, but you must first make the decision. As long as you are waffling back and forth or teetering on the fence, things will not get better or progress for you. Being indecisive not only hinders forward progress, but it impacts your effectiveness as a leader.

I understand that sometimes making the decision is the hardest thing to do. However, it is the most important step in the process. Decide today what you would like to accomplish in your career and commit to making it happen.

Remember that where you are right now in your life and your

career is a result of your decisions. However, you now have the power to make different decisions to yield different results. Will you make the decision today to do something different in your career?

Once you make the decision, commit to taking the actions necessary to see it through to completion. Next, consider multiple options for reaching your goal. Do not make the mistake of thinking that what you want can only happen in one way. Be open to the possibilities.

The Ax

After being laid off from my new job, I received a great role with the new bank. However, the role had special terms and conditions. If I did not find a new position in the company, within 18 months or my current leaders did not give the position a full-time employee (FTE) status, I would be laid off. Although in this role I still had all of my benefits and maintained my years of service, I had what I called an ax over my head. It was a constant reminder that I should not get too comfortable. I could also leave at any time and receive my full severance package.

It was an interesting position for me. Nonetheless, I was excited about the new role and grateful to be employed. I jumped in with both feet and worked hard with my team. I did not treat it any differently than any other job I previously had, and I put my all into it. However, during that time something inside of me changed. A few months before the ax was scheduled to fall, I knew it was time for me to go—to not just leave this role and this company, but to leave corporate America entirely. But what was I going to do? My career ladder plan was all I had known for so long. I had connections and my team here, yet I was not the same.

There was something about having the illusion of job security removed that caused me to see things differently. However, it took time. Although I knew that I wanted to start my own business, I did not know what that looked like so within a few months of taking time off, I started a new job. But this time my attitude and perspective were different. I did not have the same drive, focus, and aspiration that had existed in previous roles. I could not seem to get my ambition back.

In a few short months, the company announced that they were going to outsource a number of positions to India, so I ramped up my search efforts and landed a new position at a different firm. "This is the job for me," I thought. But I was wrong. Again, I did not have the drive to keep climbing my career ladder. The day when I said to my husband that I would not work a minute over 40 hours a week, I knew that something was wrong.

Not that there is anything wrong with choosing to work only 40 hours per week, but this decision and declaration was so out of line with me and my personality. I kept trying to force this to fit when it was truly time for me to do something different with my life. I had to admit to myself that I was the problem. It was not the company, the position, or the managers. It was me. Next, I had to face the fact that I needed help. I could not do this alone. So I hired a coach.

Be Still and Listen

One of the reasons why it is so difficult for us as women to make a decision is that we are far too busy. We are trying to run companies, manage households, maintain relationships, go to the gym, and shore up our sanity on an around-the-clock basis.

Oftentimes, we cram so many activities into our day that we neglect time to relax and miss out on much needed sleep. With all of this activity going on it is hard to truly know what direction to take.

As a person with a strong, hard-charging, type-A personality, I know how challenging it is to invest a few moments of quiet time in each day to gain clarity on not only the day's tasks, but the big plan as well. However, there are several risks associated with not making the time to have a quiet time of prayer or meditation each day.

The first risk is burnout. You are just too burned out to do anyone any good. When you are physically and mentally tired, you are not able to think clearly all of the time. Research shows that sleep deprivation is the same as being intoxicated.[40] You would not dare show up to work drunk, would you? But many of us superwomen do it all the time—arriving to work sleep deprived on a regular basis.

The second risk is inaction because of multiple distractions. Have you ever been in a situation when more than one person was talking to you at once? Maybe you were on the phone and someone walked in the room and struck up a conversation or maybe it was a little more animated and there were several people all vying to get to you at once. However, no matter how hard you tried to focus on what one person was saying, it was difficult to do with everyone talking at the same time. The same is true when you are over focused on several different things. Take an audit of your tasks and responsibilities. Many items on the list might be important, but are they the activities that are going to help you get to where you want to go. There is a difference between being busy and being productive. In my opinion, busyness is the number one reason why women do not achieve their goals. They allow themselves to get stuck in the same routine doing a plethora of different tasks, which distract them from pursuing their big vision. Unfortunately, they stay stuck in the same place.

Do yourself a favor and make your quiet time a priority. On your journey to shattering the inner glass ceiling, you will have to make some tough decisions, and you need to have the mental clarity to make the best possible decision you can with the information that you have available.

Delays, Detours, Disappointments, and Dead Ends

Trust me. Delays, detours, disappointments, and dead ends are all part of the journey. Someone once told me while I was working on my doctorate, "If it were easy, everyone would do it." Striving to reach the upper levels of leadership is not easy. Whether you are striving to become CEO or Area Supervisor, you will run into your share of delays, detours, and disappointments.

Cry if you must, but do not ever give up on your dream. Each no could be an opportunity for you to learn. Take time after each interview and review what went well and what could have worked better. If turned down for an opportunity, follow up with the hiring manager, if possible, to see why you were not selected. Maybe there are some skill gaps or there might be other opportunities in the future for which you are better suited.

I know of several friends and colleagues who were turned down for initial positions but were later considered for that opportunity or another opportunity within the same company. I recall a time when I was determined to move out of my current position and move away from the city where I lived. For almost a year, I had formal and informal interviews. I spoke with HR contacts and various leaders in my industry to no avail. Finally, the position I was waiting for appeared. The team flew me to Charlotte for a day of interviews. I was so excited. I went through the process, and in my opinion, did quite well. Then, I finally received the long anticipated call from the hiring manager. It had to be a good sign if he were calling me directly. He said, "Nadia, we filled the three positions, and you were number four on the list." To say that I was devastated was an understatement.

After so many months of doing what I thought was right, it only ended in such utter disappointment. I wanted to give up and throw in the towel. When I called my mentor to share the news, it took all I had to hold back the tears. However, I did not give up.

The next month, I received a call about a position in Phoenix, Arizona. Not only was this position more visible, but the salary was higher and included perks, such as full relocation. I know it is tough to hear no, especially if you hear it repeatedly, but the rewards are worth it if you stick to your plan and do not allow anyone or anything, including disappointment to cause you to give up.

Importance of Accountability

Finally, get an accountability partner. Setting goals at the beginning of a new idea or venture when you are excited is easy. But what happens after you get a few no's or hit a few bumps in the road and your excitement begins to wane? Find someone who will hold your feet to the fire. Not someone who will pet you and join you in your pity party. There is nothing like knowing I have a call coming up with my coach, and I have not done what I said I was going to do to provide that boost I need to get moving no matter how I may feel.

As you move through the various stages of your career, you will have many opportunities to opt out, back down, and play small. I know that facing some of the challenges that will come up on the journey will not be easy to overcome. Having a person to hold you accountable is so important. Find a trusted friend, mentor, or coach to help you along the way. Not only do you want someone that will hold you accountable for achieving your goals, but you want someone who will provide the needed support as you face and overcome difficult detours and delays. Knowing that you are not going at it alone may be the key to your continued growth and success.

As you continue to grow and change, the type of support you will need will change, also. Do not be afraid to get a new coach or mentor as the seasons of your life and career change. It is a natural part of the process.

How Bad Do You Want It?

No matter what your dream is, it all comes down to this simple question: How bad do you want it? When you are passionate about achieving your goals and your dream, nothing, and I mean nothing, can stand in your way. It may seem as if things are not going your way, but you must hold fast. It may not happen the way you want it, but it can happen for you. Will you commit to sticking with it through the tough times? Will you still get up after being turned down? Will you still pursue your goals even when others think they are stupid or disagree? Only you can answer those questions. One thing that I know for sure is that when people want it bad enough, they figure it out. They do not allow the lack of resources, connections, experience, or anything else stand in their way.

Being a standout female leader may not come easy. Tackling the internal glass ceiling can be challenging to overcome, however it is worth it. The decision to move forward in pursuit of your goals is up to you. Yes, there are those who do not approve of the gains that women are making and may resent your focused pursuit of your goals. However, as Eleanor Roosevelt said, "No one has the power to make you feel inferior without your consent."

Many women are stepping into their power and are making the decision to no longer remain in their designer glass cages. In a study, the fifth wave of Women, Power & Money researchers found that American women were "feeling increasingly independent, knowledgeable and successful as [they continue] growing into [their] leadership roles in the home, marketplace and workplace."[41] The findings for women in the United Kingdom, Germany, and France were similar.

Former American tennis champion and winner of 39 Grand Slam titles, Billie Jean King stated at the 2013 Fortune Most Powerful Women in London, "Pressure is a privilege. Champions adjust."[42] Consider it a privilege and honor to shatter your inner glass ceiling and lead like a lady during this time. As a standout female leader, you are able to make the adjustments necessary for your success and the success of those who will follow in your footsteps.

Final Advice from Leading Ladies

From Von:

"Go for it. Don't be timid. Find mentors. Don't get just one. Find multiple mentors and seek out mentors in different parts of the company. Be a mentor as well is important."

"My biggest flaw in my career is under networking. I got so caught up in my job and doing what I had to do that I stopped networking. I don't mean just internally within the organization, which there's a lot of connections, but I think externally. External networking is really important. Younger people today seem to do a better job of all that, but for me in my experience I would say you can't do enough of that. It is extra work; it's important. It's really important, because we get silo-ed not just within a department, but within a company. We forget that there are lots of different ways to do things, and there are a lot of different opportunities. The day may come where you might get laid off, but it also may come where you're not happy in your job. Maybe it's your boss that changes or the department changes or how you do things [may change] and if you're not networking it's so much harder to shift."

"The job itself cannot become the center of your universe. You have to stay broad. Be interconnected outside. Have other things in your life, other than just your job. Get involved in professional networking groups, especially if your company pays for that stuff. Go! Be involved. It's really important."

From Connie:
"Learn the lesson of trust. Learn to trust yourself and have confidence. Believe in every success you have and use your failures as a learning experience."

From Peatric:
"We need to educate ourselves. That's the only way we will be ahead of the curve. A degree signifies commitment and shows that you're focused, dedicated, and committed."

From Barbara:
"I can't stress enough the importance of being true to yourself and your core values. Mistakes will happen, embrace them, learn and move on always appreciating the opportunity. Laugh often. Don't take yourself too serious. Don't stay too long. Move when you need to move. Don't settle and never let anyone make you feel guilty about your choices. And finally, pay it forward. Invest in others. You may make the difference in helping someone do the impossible. Whatever you do, put your stamp on it!"

End Notes

1.   Ken Blanchard and Phil Hodges, *Lead Like Jesus* (Nashville: Thomas Nelson, 2005).

2.   Tracey Wilen-Daugenti, *Women Lead* (New York: Peter Lang, 2013).

3.   "doyenne." Merriam-Webster.com, Merriam-Webster, 2011, Web. 15 August 2011.

4.   "lady." Merriam-Webster.com, Merriam-Webster, 2013, Web. 18 March 2013.

5.   Hesse-Biber, Sharlene N. and Gregg L. Carter. *Working Women in America.* (New York: Oxford University Press, 2005).

6.   Karen S. Boyd. "Glass Ceiling" *Encyclopedia of Race, Ethnicity, and Society, Ed.* (Thousand Oaks: Sage, 2008), 549-52, http://www.sagepub.com/northouse6e/study/materials/reference/reference14.1.pdf

7.   Federal Glass Ceiling Commission, *Good for Business: Making Full use of the Nation's Human Capital* (Washington, DC: Federal Glass Ceiling Commission, 1995). http://www.dol.gov/oasam/programs/history/reich/reports/ceiling.pdf

8.   Hannah Rosin. *The End of Men: And the Rise of Women* (New York: Riverhead, 2012).

9.   Ibid.

10.   Ibid.

11.   Carter G. Woodson, *The Mis-Education of the Negro (reprint)* (Chicago: African American Images, 2000).

12.   Mohamed G. Alkadry and Leslie E. Tower, "Unequal Pay: The Role of Gender" *Public Administration Review*, November/December (2006): 888-898. http://www.library.eiu.edu/ersv-docs/4371.pdf

13.   Michelle K. Ryan and S. Alexander Haslam, "The glass cliff:

Evidence that women that women are over-represented in precarious leadership positions," *British Journal of Management* 16 (2005): 81-90

14. Hannah Rosin. *The End of Men: And the Rise of Women* (New York: Riverhead, 2012).

15. Fortune Most Powerful Women Summit. "IBM's Ginni Rometty on Taking Risks." Online Video Clip. YouTube, 5 October 2011. Web. 3 March 2013. http://www.youtube.com/watch?v=Du_a0CCJkWE

16. Institute of Leadership and Management, *Ambition and Gender at Work* (London: Institute of Leadership and Management, 2011).

17. Linda Babcock, Sara Laschever, Michele Gelfand, and Deborah Small. "Nice Girls Don't Ask," *Harvard Business Review* 81, 10 (2003, October 1):14-16.

18. Linda Babcock and Sara Laschever, Women Don's Ask: Negotiation and the Gender Divide (Princeton, NJ: Princeton University Press, 2003).

19. Ibid.

20. Collette Dowling. *The Cinderella Complex: Women's Hidden Fear of Independence* (New York: Pocket Books Publishing, 1982).

21. Valerie Young. *The Secret Thoughts of Successful Women* (New York: Crown Publishing Group, 2011).

22. Casey Mulligan. "In a First, Women Surpass Men on U.S. Payrolls." *New York Times*, 5 February 2010: Web.

23. Hannah Rosin. *The End of Men: And the Rise of Women* (New York: Riverhead, 2012).

24. Michael J. Silverstein and Katherine Sayre. "Women Want More" *Boston Consulting Group* (September 2009).

25. Catalyst. *The Bottom Line: Connecting Corporate Performance and*

Gender Diversity (New York: Catalyst, 2004).

26.   Susan Jeffers. *Feel the Fear… And do it Anyway* (New York: Ballantine Books, 2007).

27.   Hannah Seligson. Ladies, "Take off Your Tiara!" *Huffington Post*, 20 February 2007: Web.

28.   *The Pursuit of Happyness*. Gabriele Muccino. Sony Pictures, 2006. Film

29.   TED Talks. "Brené Brown: The Power of Vulnerability" Online Video Clip. TED Talks, December 2010. Web. 20 June 2013. http://www.ted.com/talks/brene_brown_on_vulnerability. html

30.   Marcus Buckingham. *First Break all the Rules* (New York: Simon & Schuster, 1999).

31.   Tom Rath. *Strengths Finder 2.0* (New York: Gallup Press, 2007).

32.   Julie Gleeson and Sherry Platt Berman. *Inside Job: 8 Secrets to Loving Your Work and Thriving* (San Francisco: Bush Street Press, 2012).

33.   Marcus Buckingham. *Find Your Strongest Life: What the Happiest and Most Successful Women do Differently* (Nashville: Thomas Nelson, 2009).

34.   Tom Rath. *Strengths Finder 2.0* (New York: Gallup Press, 2007).

35.   Michelle McQuaid. "Two-thirds America Unhappy at Job: 65% Choose New Boss Over Raise Says Study" *Business Wire*, 16 October 2012. Web

36.   Jim Giuliano. "7 Big Reasons People Leave Their Jobs" *HR Morning* 6 June 2008. Web._

37.   Thomas J. Denham. "I Don't Know What I Want, But This Ain't Doing It." accessed June 1, 2013, http://jobsearch.about.

com/od/careeradvice/a/transition.htm

38. Dennis Nishi. "You're your Search for a Job Offline" *Wall Street Journal,* 24 March 2013. Web.

39. Mirella Visser. *The Female Leadership Paradox: Power, Performance, and Promotion* (London: Palgrave Macmillan, 2011).

40. Jeffrey S. Durmer and David F. Dinges. Neurocognitive Consequences of Sleep Deprivation." *Seminars in Neurology* 25,1 (2005): 117-129.

41. FleishmanHillard, Hearst, and Ipsos. *Women, Power, & Money: Wave 5* (St. Louis: FleishmanHillard, 2013).

42. Patricia Sellers. "Gen Y Women Excel – and Learn From the Pros" *Fortune,* 2 July 2013. Web.